# Stories from
# Medieval Times

**ROSEMARY REES**
**JANE SHUTER**

Heinemann

Reed Educational and Professional Publishing Ltd Halley Court, Jordan Hill, Oxford
OX2 8EJ

MELBOURNE AUCKLAND OXFORD CHICAGO PORTSMOUTH NH IBADAN
GABORONE JOHANNESBURG

© Rosemary Rees and Jane Shuter 1998

The moral rights of the proprietors have been asserted.

First published 1998

02   01   00   99
10   9   8   7   6   5   4   3   2

British Library Cataloguing in Publication Data is available from the British Library on request

ISBN 0435 32263 X

Produced by Magnet Harlequin, Oxford

Illustrated by Stephen Wisdom

Printed in Scotland by Scotprint

*Acknowledgements*

Adaptations and extracts from the following are by kind permission of the copyright holders:
P C Doherty, *A Tournament of Murders*, Headline
Cynthia Harnett, *The Woolpack*, Methuen
Roger Lancelyn Green, *The Adventures of Robin Hood*, Puffin
A E Marston, *The Wolves of Savernake*, Headline
Ellis Peters, *The Virgin in the Ice*, Futura
Rosemary Sutcliff, *The Witch's Brat*, Oxford University Press
The publishers have made every effort to trace the copyright holders of material in this book. Any omissions will be rectified in subsequent editions if notice is given to the publisher.

# Contents

| | |
|---|---|
| The Gift | 4 |
| The Death of a Brave King | 9 |
| A Clash of Wills | 13 |
| Victims of Civil War | 16 |
| Murder! | 20 |
| The Good Spirit of Sherwood | 24 |
| The Lost Children | 28 |
| Revenge | 32 |
| Stowaway! | 35 |
| A Desperate Time | 36 |
| The Witch's Brat | 39 |
| Crisis in the Castle | 42 |
| The Reckoning | 44 |
| Death in Cuxham | 45 |
| A Glorious Victory? | 48 |
| Dangerous Words | 51 |
| Chain Reaction | 54 |
| The Woolpack | 56 |
| Harry Bailey's Inn | 60 |

# The Gift

It is the autumn of 1066. Harold, King of England, has defeated Harald Hardrada at the Battle of Stamford. He is marching south to meet the threat from William, Duke of Normandy. Duke William's ships have already put out to sea.

I knew they were there, of course. I didn't have to turn round. They were there, just as surely as my father was swearing and sweating and digging out a flooded ditch. They were there, just as surely as my mother was skinning a rabbit for supper. They were there, just as surely as my grandmother... But I didn't want to think about my grandmother. Not now, not ever.

For the moment, I had to decide what to do. Who should I warn? More to the point, who would believe me? I knew the ships were there, just over the horizon. I could feel their menace. I knew they meant us harm. Could I convince anyone? People didn't believe what they couldn't see. And by the time they could see them, it would be too late. Back to the old problem. How did I know the ships were there? I knew because of my grandmother.

My grandmother was, I suppose, the village's wise woman. People went to see her if they had warts or pustules or the black spit. She saved Guthra's baby when he was born feet first and nearly strangled himself on his cord. She put comfrey on Edgar's twisted knee and he was back driving his oxen in a couple of days. But it was more than that. She knew if the harvest was going to be good or bad; she knew

## The Gift

whether the pigs would find acorns and when the hens were going off lay. She knew, too, when death was going to come to our village. Sometimes she knew who had the mark of death on them. People said she had second sight. It was a gift, but it was a terrible gift. Last Sunday, in the middle of the Mass, two days before she died, she looked at me. She looked at me and she knew. She knew what I had been hiding for months. I had the gift, too. There, I've said it. And now I have to decide what to do with the knowledge I have of the harm that is coming to us; of the harm that is steadily advancing and is there, just over the horizon.

I made up my mind. The priest would know. He would know who to warn and how to call out the fyrd (local army). He wouldn't laugh at me. I put my knife and wood I had been carving into their hiding place in the bole of the great oak tree I was sitting in, edged carefully along the hefty branch, swung down and dropped to the ground. Then I ran, as fast as I could, feet slipping on the slippery, chalky path which wound from the edge of the Downs to our village.

The old wooden church stood by itself at the top of the village. No one spotted me as I pushed hard on the heavy door and slipped inside. I stopped for a moment to catch my breath. The familiar, sharp smell of incense and the softer smell of wood and earth surrounded me. The priest was there, on his knees before the altar. I waited. Impatient – shuffling my feet on the hard earth floor and trying not to sneeze. How long would he take? Just how long did we have? Finally, he stood up, turned to me, and held me gently by my shoulders. 'Well, well, what have we here? A grubby wood elf? What is your business, child?' Stumblingly, I told him. About knowing that ships were coming. About knowing they meant no good. About knowing that they were evil. He listened. He was good at that. And then he spoke. 'Truly you are Ella's grandchild. But I can do nothing. I will not call out the fyrd to defend Harold the oath breaker.' And he turned away, back to his business with his God.

I panicked then. The priest had believed me, but he would do nothing. I needed to find someone who would believe me and do something. Quickly. My father? By now, he would be drunk with ale and ready for his supper. He wouldn't be pleased about what I had to say. But who else was there? I ran back through the village and burst into our cottage, scattering chickens and children as I went. My mother straightened up from the fire where she had been stirring the stew. Hand on her back, she peered at me through the smoke. My little

# Medieval Times

# The Gift

brothers took no notice and just carried on rolling around and idly punching each other. My father stared at me, his eyes red from drink, tiredness and a smoking fire.

I had barely finished telling him what I knew when he roared, 'Dreamer of dreams and teller of tales! Keep me from my supper, would you! There'll be no fyrd called out because of a child's imaginings! Get to bed and your brothers will have your share of the rabbit stew! Think yourself lucky I'm not beating this stupidity out of you!'

My mother put her arm round me. 'Hush, now. You've been making up stories in your head again. And listening to what you shouldn't. You've heard too much talk from the grown-ups. There are no ships and no Duke William sailing towards us, just over the horizon. King Harold has had a great victory and is resting with his housecarls (bodyguard) in London. We are safe. Now be off with you, as your father told you.'

To my father she said, 'It would do no harm, surely, to call out the fyrd. They could do with some training, and Harold might want to call on them in an emergency…' Her voice tailed off as she caught my father's expression. 'Keep silent, woman', he bellowed. 'The fyrd in these parts number over a thousand stout Wessex men armed with staves and axes. They need no training.'

I crawled under a pile of sheepskins in the corner, which was where we children slept. I didn't cry. When you're ten years old, you don't. But those ships, with all the danger they carried, were drawing closer and closer. I was a child. I could do nothing more. I slept, but not before cursing my grandmother and the dreadful gift she had passed on to me.

Hours later, I was woken by a loud hammering on the door. The little ones screamed and my father swore. 'A-fyrd; a-fyrd', the voices shouted. And my father, pulling on his boots, half awake, staggered out into the cool dawn to join the rabble of men from our village and the surrounding hamlets who were pledged to fight for their lord. When all was quiet again, my mother came to me and put her cool face beside my hot, angry one. 'I got word,' she said, 'to Ceisig the noble. It was him who called out the fyrd. Pray to God they will be in time.'

They were in time, of course. But being in time doesn't guarantee victory. The following year, when the green shoots were again on the trees and the blue butterflies busy on the low shrubby plants of the chalky Downs, I climbed the oak tree. Would my knife and wood still be there? I pushed my hand deep into the hollow bole and pulled them out. Perhaps now I could finish carving the wooden 'W' I began so many months ago. Because I had known, you see, right from the beginning, whose head would wear the crown on Christmas Day in West Minster.

# *The Death of a Brave King*

It is 14 October 1066 and the Battle of Hastings rages on. King Harold's forces are stationed at the top of Senlac Hill and have spent the day resisting attacks by the Norman knights. Another charge by Norman knights, mounted on horseback, has just been turned back.

The young housecarl could barely contain his excitement. 'My lord, they are retreating! Victory will soon be ours!'. But Harold Godwinson, King of England, knew better. Yes it was true; the Normans were retreating. But they would be back. There was much fighting still to be done before the English could hope for victory.

All day long Harold and his brave soldiers had fought off Norman attacks, but at terrible cost. Before the battle Harold had drawn up his Saxon army on the top of Senlac Hill, hoping that the rising ground would make it more difficult for William the Conqueror's dreaded knights to launch their charges. And so it was.

Time after time the magnificent Norman horses had carried their riders up Senlac Hill to do battle with the Saxon forces. Each time Harold's men had fought them off and the Normans had retreated. Oh how the Saxons had cheered to see William's knights turn and flee! But each attack brought more casualties, more pain, more death. Young men from both sides lay dying on the battlefield, blood pouring from their terrible wounds. And, of course, beside them lay the innocent victims of the battle. The poor horses, cut down by Saxon soldiers as they fought to bring the Norman knights to ground.

The terrifying charges of the Norman knights were only part of the story. Before each attack William had ordered his archers into position at the foot of the hill. Then they had fired volley after volley of deadly arrows which rained down on the Saxon army. Harold's men were skilled in using their shields to protect themselves, but always some arrows found their target and screams of agony could be heard in the Saxon army.

'How long?' Harold wondered. How long before his army finally cracked under the relentless Norman pressure? Or was there a chance? Were the Normans suffering greater losses than his army? Were their retreats a sign from God that victory would be his? Suddenly Harold's exhaustion seemed to subside and he was filled with increased

# Medieval Times

## *The Death of a Brave King*

determination. He was the rightful King of England and no foreign invader would take his crown away!

Had he not already defeated the supposedly invincible King Harald Hardrada at Stamford Bridge? A huge Norwegian army had poured out of more than three hundred boats onto English shores and dared to challenge the King of England's authority. He had shown them! By the time the Saxon army had finished with the Norwegians they needed only 24 ships to take their miserable survivors home, leaving their own king dead on the battlefield. But Harold's joyful memories were tinged with sadness as he remembered how his own brother had joined Hardrada and had also been killed in the battle. 'Oh Tostig! You fool', he thought. 'How could you be so disloyal?'

But Harold had no time to consider the answer to this question. Instead his soldiers' shouted warnings broke into his thoughts.'Look out! Look out! They are firing again.' So the Norman archers were setting about their deadly business again. No doubt another charge would follow. Well, this one too would be resisted and more Normans would die.

Then suddenly a searing pain crashed through Harold's brain and the sky began to spin. Oh my God, the pain! The pain! Harold did not know what had happened. But the housecarls next to him stared at each other in horror. Their king was staggering and screaming in pain as an arrow had embedded itself in his right eye. He sank to his knees as the pain overcame him. His men looked on with shock as Harold tried desperately to pull the arrow from his eye.

And then came the expected Norman charge. Harold's men knew that their king was dying, but it was still their duty to protect him. But this attack seemed so much more difficult to counter than the previous ones. Could the Normans possibly know that the English king was mortally wounded? Suddenly four Norman knights broke through to where Harold lay dying. They cut down the loyal housecarls defending their king and then turned on Harold himself. Somehow the King sensed the danger and pitifully raised his shield in defence. But it was nothing more than a feeble gesture.

With the point of his lance the first knight pierced Harold's shield and penetrated his chest, his blood flowing out and drenching the ground. With his sword the second knight cut off Harold's head just below where his helmet protected him. The third knight cut out Harold's entrails, whilst the fourth hacked off one of his legs at the thigh.

## Medieval Times

At dawn the next day the women, helped by local monks, came searching amongst the dead for the bodies of their loved ones. Those looking for Harold, found him. But the sight of the mighty king's once powerful body cut to shreds horrified them. And they could only identify him by the birth mark they alone knew of. It was over. One day's battle, and a kingdom was lost.

# *A Clash of Wills*

In 1085 England was surveyed to find out how much it was worth. The following year it was surveyed again. The reading of the first survey by the second surveyors was not well received at this meeting at a village shire hall.

Canon Hubert's voice was loud in the shire hall as he read in Latin the list of who held the land in the manor made by the first Domesday survey-makers. Gervase Brett, sitting beside Canon Hubert, translated the list into English for the listeners:

'The king holds Bedwyn. King Edward held it. It never paid tax and was not assessed by hide. There is land for eighty ploughs, less one. In the lordship there are twelve ploughs and eighteen serfs. There are eighty villagers, sixty cottagers and fourteen freemen with sixty-seven ploughs between them. There are eight mills, paying one hundred shillings. There are two hundred acres of woodland and pasture twelve furlongs by six furlongs. In this manor in the reign of King Edward there was a wood held by the king. In King William's time Henry de Ferrars holds it.'

'I hear no mention of good King Harold,' challenged a Saxon voice at the back of the hall. 'Why do you have no place for him and his worth in your calculations?'

'Peace, Wulfgeat,' advised a man standing next to him.

'I asked the question of the other commissioners. They gave me no answer, either.' Wulfgeat stood up. 'I ask again, where is the record of King Harold of blessed memory?'

'He was no king,' said Canon Hubert, briskly. 'No blessing attaches to his person or his memory. We only recognise King Edward, he who was called the Confessor.'

'The noble, holy Edward,' Wulfgeat pressed on, 'left the crown to Harold on his deathbed. You cannot go against his word. And land was granted in Bedwyn by King Harold. This has to be taken into account.'

'Sit down and be silent.'

'I have just cause, I have a claim…'

'You will be heard at a time of our choosing, not now.'

'King Harold was a…'

## Medieval Times

'Usurper,' snapped Ralph, one of the commissioners, irritably. 'The crown of England was promised to Duke William of Normandy by the very Confessor whose promises you wish us to honour. We'll have no more discussion of the matter.'

He snapped his fingers and four Norman soldiers, who had been standing near the back wall, took a pace forward. The person sitting next to Wulfgeat pulled him quickly down onto his bench, hissing a warning.

Canon Hubert began to read again, Gervase to translate. At last Canon Hubert stopped. 'Thus concluded the enquiry,' he said, looking up from the heavy parchment in front of him. 'All that was recorded about the manor of Bedwyn has been read to you, as is right and proper. As you will agree, they were conscientious men, who took great care over their task.' He ignored the groans that greeted this remark.

'They were told to record the information three times.' He smiled, sharp as a knife. 'And they were asked to note if more should be given in taxes than was being given.'

The groans were louder now, and couldn't be ignored. Wulfgeat laughed contemptuously. So this was the real reason for the visit. The commissioners had come to set higher taxes. The greedy men in the Treasury had decided that Bedwyn could be squeezed harder. But far too much had already been squeezed out of them in rent and tax. If they were forced to pay more some villagers would have to give up their lands, take to the streets, starve.

The angry shouts built into a roar, until Ralph banged the table with his fist. 'Cease this noise!' he ordered. 'We are the king's commissioners. We have the right to call whoever we wish and to question them about their holdings and what they say and can pay.' He shifted his glance to the Prior of Bedwyn Abbey, sitting calmly at the front of the hall, ignoring the noise and conflict. 'Tomorrow morning, at ten o'clock, we will begin our enquiry into the lands of the Abbey of Bedwyn. Witnesses will come when called.'

The Prior sat bolt upright, and glared. Ralph beamed around the hall, pleased to have upset the Prior. 'Our business is ended for the day. We thank you for your help and your attention.'

Benches scraped the floor as the crowd rose to go. The Abbey lands were rich and there were lots of them. It might take days to make sure

## A Clash of Wills

that the charters were correct. This gave the villagers some breathing space. A group formed around Wulfgeat, clearly a leading figure in the village, whose voice was still booming mutinously as he led them out into the street.

Adapted from *The Wolves of Savernake*, by A. E. Marston.

# *Victims of Civil War*

At the time of this story, civil war was tearing England apart. It was fought between Henry I's daughter Matilda and his nephew Stephen, over who should rule after Henry died.

It was early in November of 1139 that the tide of civil war, lately so sluggish and inactive, rose suddenly to sweep over the city of Worcester. It washed away half its livestock, property and women, and sent all those of its inhabitants who could get away in time scurrying for their lives northwards away from the marauders, to burrow into hiding wherever there was manor or priory, walled town or castle strong enough to afford them shelter. By the middle of the month a straggle of them had reached Shrewsbury, and subsided thankfully into the hospitable embrace of monastery or town, to lick their wounds and pour out their grievances.

They were not in too bad case, apart from the old or sick, for the winter had not yet begun to bite hard. The weather-wise foretold that there was bitter cold in store, heavy snows and hard and prolonged frosts, but as yet the land lay dour, cloudy and mild, with capricious winds, but clear of frost or snow.

'Thanks be to God!' said Brother Edmund, the infirmarer, devoutly. 'Or we should have had more burials on our hands than three, and they all past their three score and ten.'

Even so, he was hard put to it to find beds in his hospice for all those who needed them, and there was thick straw laid down in the stone hall for the overflow. They would live to return to their spoiled city before the Christmas feast, but now, exhausted and apathetic with shock, they needed all his care, and the abbey's resources were stretched to their limits. A few fugitives with distant relatives in the town had been taken into the houses of their kin, and were warmly provided. A pregnant woman near her time had been taken, husband and all, into the town house of Hugh Beringar, the deputy sheriff of the shire, at the insistence of his wife. He had brought his wife here to the security of the town, complete with her women, midwife, physician and all, because she, too, looked forward to giving birth before the Nativity, and had a welcome for any who came in the same expectation, and in any kind of need.

## Victims of Civil War

'Our Lady,' remarked Brother Cadfael ruefully to his good friend Hugh, 'had no such reception.'

'Ah, there is but one of *my* lady! Aline would take in every homeless dog she saw in the streets, if she could. This poor girl from Worcester will do well enough now, there's nothing amiss with her that rest won't mend. We may yet have two births here for this Christmas, for she can't well be moved until she's safely over her lying-in. But I daresay most of your guests will soon be shrugging off their fears and heading for home.'

'A few have left already,' said Cadfael, 'and more of the hale ones will be off within days. It's natural they should want to get home and repair what they can. They say the king is on his way to Worcester with a strong force. If he leaves the garrison better found, they should be safe over the winter. Though they'll need to draw stores from eastwards, for their own reserves will all have been carried off.'

Cadfael knew from old experience the look, the stench, the desolation of a gutted town, having been both soldier and sailor in his young days, and seen service far afield. 'And besides wanting to reclaim what's left of their store before Christmas,' he said, 'there's the spur of the winter coming. If the roads are cleared of bad customs now, at least they can travel dry-shod and warm enough, but another month, another week it may be, and who knows how deep the snow will be?'

'Whether the roads are cleared of bad customs,' said Beringar in wary reflection, 'is more than I should care to say. We have a pretty firm hold here in Shropshire - thus far! But there's ominous word from east and north, besides this uneasiness along the border. Then the king is all too busy in the south, and his mind on where his Flemings' next pay is to come from, and his energy mostly wasted in wavering from one target to another, ambitious men in remoter parts are liable to begin to spread their honours into palatines, and set up kingdoms of their own. And given the example, the lesser fry will follow it.'

Extract from *The Virgin in the Ice,* by Ellis Peters.

# Medieval Times

## Victims of Civil War

# *Murder!*

It is 29 December 1170. King Henry II and the Archbishop of Canterbury, Thomas Becket, had quarrelled. Henry is supposed to have raged, 'Who will rid me of this turbulent priest?' Four knights decided to do what they thought Henry wanted.

I crouched down behind the huge column, its stone cold on my face. I could just make out the empty nave, stretching from the huge oak doors to the altar. This was the great cathedral at Canterbury, and I was hiding, terrified out of my mind. Odd, wasn't it, to be afraid in the house of God? Gradually my eyes adjusted to the dim light. Silently, a choir monk entered with a glowing taper in his hand and lit the candles around the altar. That was better. But couldn't he hear the noise outside, the shouting and the pleading, the crash of sword on stone? Perhaps he was more involved with God than with the clamour and sounds of hate outside.

Suddenly Archbishop Thomas was there, striding towards his altar, surrounded by whispering, pleading monks. 'Here, noble Thomas, here, quick, into this store room. There you will be safe.' 'No, no, no, Father, here, up these stairs. We will guard them. There you will be safe.' Brother James and Brother Marc, quicker thinkers than the rest put together, moved swiftly back to the great oak doors, pulled them closed and dragged the heavy iron bar into place across them. It would take King Henry's army, not just a few maddened knights, to break those doors down. I began to relax. I didn't know about Archbishop Thomas, but I certainly began to breathe more easily.

Then the incredible happened. Freeing himself from the pleading monks, Thomas turned and shouted down the length of the nave to Brother Marc and Brother James, 'Unbolt the doors. This is a house of prayer, not a fortress.' They must have had to remind themselves several times that they had taken a vow of obedience, for it was some minutes before, slowly and reluctantly, the vast doors swung open. The terrified monks had managed to push and pull their Archbishop up a flight of stone steps, and when the enraged knights rushed into the dim, cool cathedral, he was nowhere to be seen. Their harsh voices rang out, 'Where is Thomas, traitor to the king and to the realm?' 'Thomas, come out, you traitor!' 'Where is the Archbishop?'

## *Murder!*

Then Thomas appeared, calm and collected. 'I am here, no traitor to the king, but a priest. Why do you seek me?' He walked slowly to the altar, the knights shouting and clattering behind him in their armour. He turned to face them, and I have to say they did have the grace to look a bit ashamed. It was hardly the way to behave in a cathedral. Or anywhere else, for that matter. Then one of the knights began shouting again. 'Forgive,' he yelled. 'Absolve those bishops you barred from the Church and who are excommunicated.' I kept my fingers crossed here, I can tell you. All Thomas had to do was agree and we could all go home. Not very likely.

'No,' he said, firmly and clearly. 'They have done nothing to show they have repented of choosing their king instead of their God.'

'Then you shall die. Die, die', they yelled, beside themselves with fury. All the time the wretched monks were standing trembling and crossing themselves. You'd have thought they would have tried to stop the knights. There were more monks than knights, after all. I was just a cleaner. I wasn't expected to do anything. I wouldn't have been there at all if I hadn't been stupid enough to come back for my leather bucket.

'I am ready to die', said Thomas calmly. 'I am ready to die for my Lord so that, through my blood, the Church may obtain peace. But in the name of Almighty God I forbid you to hurt my people, whether clerk or lay.' Well, that was something, at least. Maybe I would get out of this dreadful mess alive.

The knights grabbed Thomas and tried to drag him out of the cathedral. I suppose they didn't want to kill him on sacred ground. But he hung on to a pillar – just opposite the one I was hiding behind. There was no way he was going to let go. That man was determined to die in his own cathedral. One of the knights raised his sword high in the air. He was going to bring it down on Thomas' head. Suddenly Brother Edward Grimm, the best of the lot, flung himself between the knight and the Archbishop. It was too late. The sword flashed down, slicing off the top of Thomas' head and embedding itself in Brother Edward's arm. There was screaming and blood and one of the voices was my own. A second blow to Thomas' head, but he was still standing, blood pouring down his face and robe and making a dark pool on the ground. It was the third blow which felled him. A sword sliced through his head and broke against the stone floor. Then all the knights moved in and I couldn't see much except a dreadful white slime oozing out of the smashed skull. The knights stepped back and I saw,

# Medieval Times

## *Murder!*

horror upon horror, Hugh the sub-deacon, who was supposed to be a man of God, put his foot on Thomas' neck. With the point of his sword, Hugh picked Thomas' brains out of his poor, smashed head. I was suddenly and violently sick and through a red mist, I heard him shout, 'Let us away, knights. He will rise no more.'

# *The Good Spirit of Sherwood*

How real are the stories of Robin Hood? No one knows for sure – he left no trace. But Prince John was real, he did rule in King Richard's absence, and he was cruel and ruthless. If Robin Hood was the man of his legend, Prince John would have wanted to capture him.

John was a cruel, merciless man, and most of his followers were as bad as he. They needed money, and he needed money: the easiest way of getting it was to accuse some wealthy man of treason or law-breaking, make him an outlaw – and seize his house or castle and all his goods. For an outlaw could own nothing, and anyone who killed him would be rewarded.

When Prince John had seized a man's lands he would usually put one of his own followers in his place – provided he paid him large sums of money. Prince John's followers did not mind how they came by this money: for them the easiest way was to take it from the small farmers, the peasants and even from the serfs. And not only Prince John's upstart knights and squires did this, but many also of the Bishops and Abbots who were either in league with him, or greedy for their own good like the worst of the nobles and barons.

Many a Sheriff, too, was appointed to keep order and administer justice in the towns and counties by Prince John – provided he paid well for the honour: and of course he had also to force the money from someone weaker than himself, and obey Prince John however cruel and unjust his orders might be.

Such a one was the Sheriff of Nottingham, the little town on the edge of Sherwood Forest, and when Prince John came and set up his Court there for a time, he was naturally most eager to show his loyalty and zeal.

One evening he and his men came upon a serf who had killed a deer. Without a thought of pity, the Sheriff ordered the poor man's cottage to be searched for money, and when none was found, had it burnt to the ground.

Then the wretched serf was brought before him.

## The Good Spirit of Sherwood

'You know the Forest Laws,' said the Sheriff grimly. 'All right, my men: one of you heat the irons quickly. Blind him, and turn him loose!'

'No, no! Not that!' shrieked the man. 'Anything but that! Kill me straightaway! If you blind me God will repay you! Mercy! Mercy!'

Prince John had ridden out to see the Sheriff at work, and at this moment he joined the little group round the glowing embers of the cottage.

'What night-jar have we here?' he asked carelessly. 'Surely, good Sheriff, you should have cut out his tongue first. You should keep silent and secret if you expect this bogey Robin Hood to come to his aid, as I've heard tell he does. Why, this man's cries will waken the King in Palestine, or wherever he is now!'

'Silence, you dog!' cried the Sheriff, striking the serf roughly across the mouth. 'You ought to know better than to make this unseemly noise in the presence of His Royal Highness Prince John!'

'Prince John! Prince John!' gasped the man. 'Oh, save me, sire! For God's love, save me!'

'Who is he?' asked John casually. 'What has he done?'

'They call him Much,' said the Sheriff importantly. 'He was a miller once. But he was too fond of the King's deer. See, his first and second fingers have been cut off: that tells its own story – a bowstring pulled unlawfully. Now we've caught him at it again: the law lays it down that for a second conviction for deer-slaying, a man shall have his eyes burnt out. A third time – and he hangs. But I'll warrant he'll find it hard to shoot a deer when we've done with him: I've never known a man to shoot by smell – ha! ha!'

The Sheriff laughed heartily at his own joke, and Prince John was pleased to smile.

'Well, fellow?' he said to poor old Much, who still knelt trembling before him.

'So please your highness,' gasped Much, 'they burnt my mill to make a wider hunting-ground and a way to the stream so that the deer could come there to drink. How could I get my food but hunting? It's hard to shoot straight and true lacking the arrow fingers, and true and straight must a man shoot if he would kill lawful game, the rabbit and the wood-pigeon… I had two children, one died of want, and my boy,

# Medieval Times

young Much was crying out for food... We cannot live long upon grass and herbs like an ox, nor upon the roots that the swine eat.'

'Oh,' said Prince John, 'so you decided to try a richer diet, did you? The king's deer!... Was there no other way? No, no, Master Sheriff, let me deal justly with him... What of this Robin Hood of whom tales are told? Some rich man, they say – a yeoman or a nobleman born of some old Saxon family – who, mad fool, brings help to such dirt as you and your kin of law breakers, kills the king's deer himself, and has even robbed a purse on the highway before now... Well, where is he? And, more to the point, who is he? Tell me that, and you shall keep your eyes to see your way to the gallows one day, I'll be bound!'

'I know not who he is!' gasped Much. 'Robin Hood comes out of the forest – men say he is the Good Spirit of Sherwood – and having brought help, he goes away as silently as he came. No one has seen him by daylight...'

'Faugh!' cried Prince John impatiently. 'Take him away and do your work on him out of my sight. These rogues are too loyal for my liking, or for their own good.'

So four of the Sheriff's men dragged poor Much away while a fifth drew the glowing irons from the fire which had been his home and followed grimly at his heels. But suddenly with a desperate cry he tore himself loose, snatched a sword from one of them, and made a rush at Prince John. He never reached him, however, for with a sudden vicious whine an arrow sped from behind them and laid him dead on the ground.

'A good shot, truly,' remarked Prince John, 'though I could wish that it had

## The Good Spirit of Sherwood

but maimed him. A dead man is no bait for this Robin Hood... Who was it loosed this arrow?'

He turned as he spoke, and saw advancing towards him from the edge of the glade a short dark man wearing a green cloak over his suit of brown leather.

'My lord,' said the man, bowing very low before Prince John, 'I am called Worman, Steward to Robert Fitzooth, Earl of Huntingdon.'

Extract from *The Adventures of Robin Hood*, retold by Roger Lancelyn Green.

# *The Lost Children*

Since 1196 Christian Crusaders had fought holy wars against the Muslims over control of the holy city of Jerusalem. The Children's Crusade to Jerusalem was one of the most unusual events of the time.

'I saw Jesus,' the boy was yelling. 'He was dressed as a poor pilgrim, but I know it was him. He spoke to me. "Stephen," he said, "you must gather up the children and march to save the city of Jerusalem. Come with me! Come now! God wants us to go!" '

I felt excitement tugging at my heart. Stephen was just a shepherd, twelve years old, only a year older than me. But why should God not speak to him? We were told over and over in church that God loved children and had a special care for them. I knew I had to join them in the march to Jerusalem.

My mother wept. Of course she did – mothers do. 'Don't go,' she begged. 'Children can't fight trained soldiers! How can you even make the long journey? How will you eat, where will you sleep? Oh, Will, do not go!'

But in the end she made me up a bundle of food and clean clothes and gave me as much money as she could find.

So I found myself walking behind Stephen's cart, all decorated with flowers and strips of bright cloth, as we set out from our tiny village near Orléans in France to march to the port of Marseilles. It felt wonderful. We all felt so sure of success! We sang hymns as we went and Stephen called out: 'Join us! We are on a holy crusade. God will protect us, and we will get our reward in Heaven.'

Children working in the fields dropped their tools and ran to join us; they didn't even stop to tell their parents. Word of our crusade spread far and wide. Children joined us from all over France, and even from Germany! It got so that there were so many of us you couldn't see the road.

Some people in the villages along the way blessed us and gave us food and shelter. But not everyone supported us. Parents of children who were joining us tried to stop them – to stop all of us. Even the King of France sent messengers to tell us: 'You have not been trained to fight. The crusades need fit and healthy knights. Go back to your homes and

## *The Lost Children*

families. You have shown your love for God by coming this far, but go no further. Go home.'

But we kept on. Our duty to God was greater than our duty to the King.

Marseilles was huge, crowded, dirty, noisy and smelly. We had to get across the sea to the Holy Land, but how? We hadn't enough money between us to hire one ship, never mind all the others we would need to take all of us. But Stephen wasn't downhearted. 'God will provide,' he said, confidently.

And then God did provide, or so it seemed. If only we had known better. Two merchants came to us, Iron Hugh and William the Pig. They offered us seven ships to cross the sea to the Holy Land. 'We believe in your crusade,' they told Stephen. 'We want to help you, and you don't have to pay us. We will get our reward.'

And they did. We thought they meant they would get their reward in Heaven. It turned out they had a much more earthly reward in mind.

We all piled into the ships. I had never seen the sea before, much less been on it. It felt very strange to have the world unsteady under my feet. We were crowded together, but we didn't mind. The most important thing was to get as many of us across the sea as we could. The ships set sail. Stephen was in the first boat, I was in the third. Then disaster. A storm blew up, out of nowhere. The ships were tossed about by the waves, seawater poured over the sides and down below the decks. It was a nightmare. Most of us were seasick – vilely, revoltingly sick. The captain and his crew kept us bailing out the water, bailing for our lives. They drove us on with curses and blows, until the storm gave way. In the calm of the storm we found that some of the younger ones had been washed overboard and drowned. And there was worse. The last two ships, the fullest and least able to ride out the storm, had sunk entirely. The sea around us was full of bodies.

Worse followed. The ships lost sight of one another and when we arrived at port one of the children asked a sailor: 'Where are the other ships? How soon will they get here? How far is it now, to Jerusalem?'

'It won't matter to you now how far Jerusalem is,' the sailor replied. 'Your journey ends here, where you're going to make William the Pig a fat profit!'

'What do you mean?'

# Medieval Times

'You'll find out soon enough, now get ashore.'

We did find out. The crew herded us ashore and we were split up into groups, with brothers and sisters being separated for the first time in their lives. The next day my group of about twenty children were sold in the marketplace – sold as slaves to make a profit for William the Pig.

❈ ❈ ❈

My master is a Moor, a follower of Islam, one of the very infidels that Stephen called on us to fight. But he is not a devil. He is not even a bad man. He is a doctor, and is kind enough to me. He works me hard, mixing his potions and ointments, cleaning his home. But he feeds me

# The Lost Children

well and I have a bed in the corner of the kitchen. I am becoming used to my new home in the Holy Land, used to the heat, the different smells of the night air, even the language.

I know I am one of the lucky ones. Many of those who were sold are probably dead by now, beaten to death, or worse. Sometimes I wonder what happened to Stephen, whether he is still alive, and if he is, whether it is worse for him, knowing what he brought us to, knowing the failure of his dream. At other times I wonder if I will ever be free, ever be able to get home and see my parents once more before they die.

# *Revenge*

After Edward I's English army defeated the Welsh in 1282 he set about building castles throughout the country so that he could control the people. Many people in Wales bitterly resented being ruled and controlled by outsiders.

The castle rises, day by day, built out of the solid, reddish stone of our Welsh hills. But it isn't our castle, no! It is the castle of the enemy and it is built to keep us out, to keep us down, to keep us bowing and scraping to the Norman invaders.

I was very young when the Normans took over. I can remember the men of our village going away to fight with David ap Gryffyd in the hills. I remember that only some of them came home – dirty, sullen, starved and beaten. My father was not with them. He never came back, and they never spoke of their time away, ever, unless it was among themselves, out of anyone else's hearing. I believe they never spoke about it because they were ashamed. Though why they should be ashamed I cannot understand. They fought as well as they could for as long as they could, and good men have been beaten before, and will be again I've no doubt.

But I did blame them for the way they behaved towards the Normans. They were sullen and unhelpful, but they did not resist. All the fight had gone out of them. No one did anything when Edward's men just marched in and knocked down the Abbey where Llewelyn the Great was buried. It was as if the conquerors were saying, 'Here I am, and here I stay, and I can do as I please and you just have to put up with it!'

And they did put up with it. It's bad enough that the great castle rises, casting its huge shadow over us. It's worse that they put it there. This is where the greatest of our Welsh kings was buried, and they just shovelled his bones aside. But what could we have done? Had we done anything they would have burned our homes, mistreated our women and children, and seized our animals. The enemy doesn't feel secure enough to let us get away with the merest offence. They are heavy-handed over the least thing.

The soldiers are already pacing the walls, looking down over the town watching us. All they can see are people who are beaten and starving. We are short of food and supplies because we can't trade, except when the enemy lets us. The carts arrive with food and supplies for them and they help themselves to whatever we have that they need.

## Revenge

There is talk that once the castle is built they will fill the town with people who will be more loyal to them, people who will watch us for them, people who will run the town for them. But that may be just talk.

Some of the castle builders are Welsh, but many are English. The English who can speak Welsh talk to the children who watch the castle rise, give them apples, call the little ones 'Cariad, darling,' and talk about how they themselves have little ones at home. But how would they like it if our men were building a castle beside their town? They may be friendly, but they are not our friends.

I have a plan. Already it's taking shape. I watch the builders and talk to them. I am still young enough to be a child in their eyes – innocent and above suspicion. But maybe old enough to be suspected if I fall in with them too fast. So I have gone slowly. A sullen word or two, here and there. I pretend to be drawn to the castle despite myself, which is not hard to do. Slowly I have let them believe that I trust them, when in fact I have been gaining theirs. Now they let me help a bit, after all I'm a handy young lad, strong and able. But not able to move the biggest stones, not a danger, not a problem. Not yet.

This is how I managed to find out so much about their plans for the castle. It's big, but its garrison will be small, only thirty or so men. Thirty men! That's nothing. Thirty men can be so easily killed. They are relying on the castle to keep them safe, the castle with its high pinkish brown walls, its ditches, its drawbridge, to shut the enemy out. But what if the enemy was in? A garrison of so few men might well want a boy to fetch and carry for them. Maybe one or two. And who do they trust already? Who do they know by his first name? Who have they taught to say 'Good morning' in their barbarous tongue? Who better than little Geraint Hughes? Me.

As time passes they will get less suspicious. They will relax their guard, just a bit. They will doze on guard duty, maybe even sleep. Just thirty men, including the cook and the priest and a few builders to keep the repairs going. And one insignificant boy who will have watched how the drawbridge works, who will have watched to see who sleeps, who sneaks off to sit by the fire in the kitchen when he should be on the walls. A boy who has all the patience to wait until the time is right to let down the drawbridge and let in the enemy, to take this castle, made from our stone, into our own hands.

# Medieval Times

# *Stowaway!*

My father hates me, and who could blame him? I was, until last week, apprenticed to a cooper. I loathed it. Who wants to spend their life making wooden barrels? So, I walked out. My father had paid a lot of money to get me apprenticed to a master cooper. That is all lost. I am the oldest and he has five other kids to think about. He's thrown me out and I have to fend for myself. But I know what I'm going to do. I've been watching this ship all day. I know about barrels. I know where they're stacked in the hold and how they are stacked. There are gaps in between. And when it's dark, I'm going to slip aboard and hide. Once we're out at sea, the ship won't turn back. I'll work my passage and see what I can find, away from this place.

# *A Desperate Time*

When Edward I's army defeated Robert the Bruce's forces at Methven, the Scottish king escaped to the safety of the Highlands. Having failed to capture Robert, the English instead took his wife and daughter and his sisters.

This prison stinks. There are rats in the straw. I am sure of it. You can hear them rustling. My mother is wailing in a corner and I am sitting wondering at what has happened to our family in these last few months. We have been swept along from one event to the other, ever since my father was crowned King of Scotland some four months ago.

'Be proud, Marjory,' my aunt Isabella said.
'Your father is getting his rightful dues at last,' my aunt Mary added.

The English king marched against father, at once. Everyone must have realised this would happen. It had never occurred to me. If my father had got what was rightfully his, why should anyone take it away?

## *A Desperate Time*

'The English are greedy for land.'
'The English are greedy for power.'
'The English must be taught a lesson.'
'The English must be beaten in battle.'

This was the talk around the table. Fighting talk. And who else could lead the Scots into battle but their newly crowned king? So father left, and mother cried, and so did I.

'Elizabeth, you must get away, go somewhere safe,' father said to my mother. 'Take Marjory and go to Kildrummy Castle. You should be safe enough there. The King of England has no quarrel with an innocent woman and a twelve-year-old girl. Pack and go quickly.'

Even then I wondered why we had to go at all if it was true that the English king had no quarrel with us. We went to Kildrummy. We had not been there many weeks when my mother told me to pack. 'We have to go to a safer place,' she said. 'Our army has been defeated at Methven. The survivors have been forced to flee to the mountains. God knows what will become of them, or us if we are caught! How will your father manage in the mountains when winter comes?'

'I thought father said we would be safe here?'

'We are in a castle guarded by Scots, in a country invaded by the English. No castle is safe. Any castle is a challenge to the English army. We will go to Tain. There is a place there, dedicated to St Duthac, which is a holy place of safety for those in trouble. We will be safe there.'

So we went to Tain. Even so the English found us and not even the holiness of our hiding place could save us being taken captive at sword point. Our captors marched us, mile by weary mile, through Scotland and into England. And here we are, strangers in a foreign country.

Those guarding us make fun of us. 'Cold enough for you?' they ask, knowing that the people in Scotland are now living through the bitterest winter in living memory and my father and his men are penned up in the freezing mountains. They just laugh when I shout at them. 'Got her father's temper, not much good it will do her,' they say. 'She'll end up like her aunties one of these days, you mark my words!'

Poor Isabella and Mary. They were made an example of. Isabella was taken to the city of Berwick, Mary to Roxburgh. Each of them was penned in an iron cage – cages so small they could barely move. The

## Medieval Times

cages were then hung from the city walls of Berwick and Roxburgh so that the people could clearly see them hanging there. Guards mocked the caged women and pelted them with fruit and stones. They were left there to freeze, to starve, to die, to rot. You can be sure that our guards keep us well informed of every turn in the women's misery.

'We are not so badly off,' my mother says, on her good days. 'We are alive. The King of England will not kill us in case your father lives to come down the mountain and rally the Scots to him.'

'What will the English king do then?'

'He'll tell Robert he has us in his grip. He'll threaten to harm us if your father doesn't give in.'

'So what will father do?'

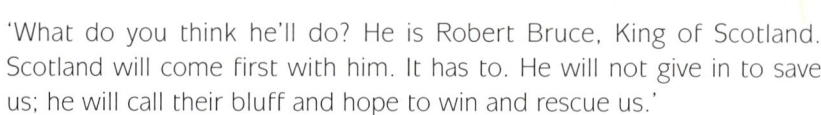

'What do you think he'll do? He is Robert Bruce, King of Scotland. Scotland will come first with him. It has to. He will not give in to save us; he will call their bluff and hope to win and rescue us.'

So here we sit and wait for winter to pass. What do I wish for? I want father to be alive, safe. I don't want him to be captured, humiliated, killed. I want him and his army to come down from the mountains, safe. I want them to rally an army and fight the English, and win a glorious victory. I want all of us to be together again. But I am twelve years old, too old for fairy stories.

# *The Witch's Brat*

Lovel was a handicapped boy (nicknamed 'the witch's brat') who fled in terror from his village. Monks in a nearby monastery took him in and cared for him. When he recovered, he looked after their garden.

The sunlit, longshadowed peace of the early summer evening was scattered by a shower of excited barks, and Lovel grinned to himself as he hoed carefully round the roots of a rosemary bush. Valiant was after the stable cat again! But almost in the same instant the barking changed to an agonized yelping, and there was a shout and flurry of voices. Lovel dropped the hoe and headed at a limping run for the little door in the high wall, almost hidden by a buttress of the church, dragged it open and stumbled out into the great forecourt.

The hay-cart stood in the middle of the open space, with the horse backing and fidgeting uneasily in the shafts; a little group of men were gathered beside it, and in their midst, Valiant, yelping and yelping in pain and bewilderment, was trying to struggle up on three legs.

Harding had come running from the stables, and people were talking all at once: 'Ran right under the wheels!' – 'Always did say he'd chase that cat once too often.'

And the loudest voice of all was Jehan's, saying, 'It's broken. Best knock him on the head and be done with it.'

Lovel saw the look on their faces – the look on Harding's face above all – and shouted, 'No! Wait!' And next moment he was in the midst of the group, pushing his way through to where Valiant, quiet now, crouched on three legs with his head distressfully down, and his right foreleg half tucked up at a queer unnatural angle. 'Hold him for me, Harding,' he said; and got down awkwardly on to his sound knee and held out a reassuring hand, 'Easy, boy. Easy, Valiant, let me look.'

'Look out, he'll bite,' somebody said. 'He won't bite me. He's got too much sense, and he knows I'm trying to help him.' Lovel's hands were on the place now; he could feel the break in the bone. Valiant was shuddering from head to tail, but he made no sound, and certainly no attempt to snap. Lovel went on feeling very carefully and gently at the broken bone, and talking reassuringly to Valiant all the time. He seemed to be seeing with his hands as well as feeling; it was all very odd. After a few moments he looked up at Harding, 'It's a clean break. If we could

# Medieval Times

get the ends to stay together and keep it straight long enough it ought to mend.'

The weatherbeaten face of the old man-at-arms was wretched and torn with doubt. 'Can we do that? I'd not want the old lad to suffer, and all to no good in the end.'

Lovel was silent a moment. He had to decide, with the dog's beautiful amber brown eyes on his face, and warm wet tongue suddenly curling out to lick his hand, whether he could really make the broken leg mend properly; or whether it would be kinder if Harding were to use his knife now, and make it all over for Valiant without any more pain. 'I think so,' he said at last. 'I'm sure it's worth trying, even if it hurts him quite a lot. Please, Harding, let me try.'

Harding looked down at his dog and then up again at the boy, and nodded. 'Tell me what you'd have me do.'

'Go on holding him like that so that he can't move about,' Lovel said; and then to the knot of bystanders, 'I'll need some straight sticks, and rags – plenty of rags, torn into strips.' And the surprising new authority was in his voice too.

Somebody laughed, and said, 'Hark to the Father Infirmarer!' But the sticks and a handful of rags were brought all the same. He chose the

## The Witch's Brat

three best bits of wood for his purpose, thin but strong, and cut them to the length he wanted with somebody's knife; then while Harding supported the broken foreleg, he began to bind them on with the strips of rag so that they held the break splinted and secure.

When the last knot was tied, Lovel sat back on his heel and thrust the hair out of his eyes, and looked about him at the outside world that he had just remembered.

He said, 'I think that'll hold, so long as we can keep him from biting at the rags. If I go now I can maybe get word with the Father Infirmarer before he goes to refectory, and ask for some comfrey, and we'll give it to him in warm milk.'

Lovel found Brother Peter in the Infirmary still-room, measuring out a syrup for Brother Godwyne's cough, and burst out with his request.

'Broken foreleg, eh,' said Brother Peter, setting down the measuring glass. 'I'm sorry to hear that, very sorry. A good friendly beast, yes, yes, and behaved as reverendly as any Christian, the time he got into the church. Comfrey, yes, I think we might spare –'

Brother Eustace's dry voice sounded from the inner doorway, 'Brother Peter, may I remind you that nothing is dispensed from the Infirmary still-room without my leave?'

'Yes, yes – of course I would have asked you before –' Brother Peter began guiltily, and his voice trailed away, as the dry one went on.

'The remedies on these shelves are for the healing of men and women and children, not for brute beasts, no matter how Christianly they behave themselves in church after they have chased the stable cat half-way up the rood screen!'

'But we have plenty of the infusion, Brother Eustace; don't you think –'

'That is beside the point,' said Brother Eustace, and his voice took on the familiar edge of exasperation. 'It's not even as though the animal was a working dog; it's a useless creature, anyway.'

Lovel suddenly heard a voice that did not seem to be quite his own, saying, 'Father Infirmarer, you said that about me, once, but I reckon you've found me useful enough to you these past months.'

Extract from *The Witch's Brat,* by Rosemary Sutcliff.

# Crisis in the Castle

There's a crisis here. Just look at what is happening. The lord and his lady are quarrelling; the feast is far from ready; and in the kitchens everything is in turmoil. At the same time, strangers are hammering on the doors and someone seems to be trying to rescue the prisoners from the dungeon.

I'm only the cook. No one tells me what's happening. Here I am, trying to get a decent feast together. The orange won't stick in the mouth of the boar's head and the wretched dog has run off with the leg of mutton. To make matters worse, Padraig has just told me there's chaos in the Hall and my lord and lady are shouting at each other in the solar. I haven't seen Edwin and that girl Ceithra all day and no one's come to ask for food for the prisoners. Two minutes ago Berit rushed in, white as a snowdrop, shouting something daft about enemies at the gate. I sent him away with a flea in his ear, I can tell you. By the finger bones of Saint Oswy, it will be a miracle if any food gets on the table today.

# Crisis in the Castle

# *The Reckoning*

It was all my fault, of course. I sat, hunched, on the floor, knees under my chin, arms hugging my knees. It was always, 'Look after your little sister.' 'You are the oldest – you should know better.' My mother's words rung in my ears, as they had done that morning and every other morning for five years. And because I hadn't listened, because I, too, had wanted to be a child and carefree, Annis was lying, still and pale, in our parents' bed. They had called the physician, of course. They were rich and could afford it. And Guy had come, tutt-tutting and shaking his head, with his great wooden box full of drawers and little bottles. He terrified me, with his long, greasy grey hair, pointy nose and button-black eyes. He shuffled about the room, muttering to himself. He threw handfuls of sweet herbs onto the fire, which hissed and spluttered. The room smelled suddenly spicy and sweet at the same time. And it got hotter and hotter until I thought I would suffocate. Still Annis did not move. Guy began mashing up a raw onion and treacle. Was Annis supposed to eat that, or have it spread on her chest and arms? I felt sick. Then Guy held up a flask with some of Annis' urine in it. He peered at his charts – would they tell him what was wrong with her? Would he know what had happened?

I rocked backwards and forwards, wishing, wishing, wishing as hard as I could that I had never pushed the door of the great hall open, grabbed Annis' hand, rushed out into the sunlit yard and...

# *Death in Cuxham*

So few survived the Black Death when it struck the village of Cuxham in 1349 that some of those still alive had to bury their own families themselves.

The priest died today. Now over half the people in our village are dead. I know the priest is dead, because I saw Robert Heycroft in the churchyard, digging away like a man possessed. The sweat was pouring off him, though that might have been the sickness. It takes some that way. He was crying – great tearing sobs, like he would go out of his mind. Next to him were the bodies of Agnes and little Robert, his two children. They were stiff and covered in the big purple bruises of the sickness.

'Stay away!' he shouted, when he saw me. 'Keep back, John, for the love of God!' And then, in a lower tone, but I could still hear him, he sobbed, 'What will happen to my babes without a proper burial, will God still take care of their souls?'

I thought of Agnes and Robert as I had last seen them, happy and laughing, playing with the rest of us village children in the big mill pond. 'God will care for them, Master Heycroft,' I said, hesitantly. 'He must know that you can do no more than what you are doing.'

'And if he had cared for them, John, do you think he would have let them die like this? Do you think he would let the sickness take the good with the bad, the old with the young, the strong with the weak? Do you think he would let the sickness fall so hard upon the churchmen who serve him? Do you think he would let all our prayers go unanswered? First my wife, now my children. ... No man should have to bury his children with his own hands. I will be next. ... And who will bury me, John East, answer me that. I will be left to lie and rot and the crows will feed on me, as they do on the dead sheep in the fields.'

There was a long silence. It was clear that Robert Heycroft was running mad with grief, and what comfort could I offer him? I could not bring his wife and children back to life. I could not answer any of his questions about the sickness, or God's part in it. There was only one thing I could do for him, and that, in Christian charity, I had to do. 'I will bury you, Master Heycroft, you have my word. I will see that you lie beside your family, as long as I have the strength to do it,' I promised.

He stared at me, gravely. 'Thank you for that,' he said. 'I will soon be holding you to your word.' Then he turned back to his awful task.

# *Medieval Times*

I went back home. I sat by the table in our cottage and thought about what Master Heycroft had said. I thought about the months that the sickness had been at Cuxham. Our family was the first to be hit. People said later that the sickness came with the bolt of red cloth that our Matilda bought from a travelling peddler. She always loved a bright piece of cloth. She was buried in it. But how could cloth bring harm?

The truth is that no one knows how the sickness came, nor how it spreads, nor how to cure it. But we know the signs. Oh yes, we know the signs. We have had practice enough by now. We have made an art of watching each other for them. The flushed cheeks, the fever, the vomiting, we watch for that. And then we leave those who are sick alone, friend or foe, it makes no difference. Family, even. Some even leave their families from fear. Then we wait. The next sign is the lumps in the armpits or groin, then the creeping horror of the black and purple bruises. Then we are sure. The Devil has laid his mark on you, you have the sickness for sure and you will die.

I am the only one to have had the sickness and recover. Everyone else in the village who has fallen sick has died. And now people have begun to talk.

# Death in Cuxham

'Why John East?'

'What did he do to live, has he made a promise to the Devil, to stay alive?'

'He must have, why else is he alive?'

'Perhaps God has chosen to show him special favour.'

'Perhaps he has a cure, that he will not share with us?'

'If that were so, why would he not have saved his family?'

'He may not have had enough. Or he may just have wanted them to die.'

I do not know why I have been spared. But I know that, whether they think I am a devil or a saint, the people of Cuxham do not want me here. And there is nothing here for me to stay for, nothing. My family are gone. At eleven, I have not yet got a sweetheart. The nearest to that was Agnes Heycroft, sweet, pretty Agnes, who is, by now, lying in the churchyard with her mother and brother. I will leave Cuxham and find a life elsewhere. There is nothing more to keep me here. But first I must wait for Master Heycroft to die, and keep my promise to him.

# *A Glorious Victory?*

During the Hundred Years War the English and French armies fought a bloody battle at Poitiers in France. The English were victorious, but there was a price to pay.

In a muddy ditch beneath a hedgerow, Sir Gilbert Savage, a poor knight, lay gasping as the blood seeped through his armour, forming a dark-red pool around him. In the gathering darkness his squire, Richard Greenele, tried to make him comfortable.

'I should undo your straps, Sir Gilbert, at least tend the wound.' He peered down at the knight's face. 'Shall I fetch a doctor?'

'Damn all their eyes!' Sir Gilbert whispered. 'Let me at least die with dignity, in my armour.' He caught Richard's wrist in a surprisingly firm grip, and pulled himself up. 'Listen,' he hissed. 'No priest, no doctor. Richard, you are to leave the battlefield now.'

'Now?' the young squire replied. 'But Sir Gilbert ...'

'The battle is finished,' the older man replied.
'The Black Prince has his victory.'

## *A Glorious Victory?*

'What will happen to you?' Richard asked. 'Your possessions, your...'

'What possessions?' Sir Gilbert laughed, softly. 'Some battered armour. A horse now dead. A few pennies in my purse?' He reached down, dragged up his saddlebags from by his side. 'After years of duty in one castle and another, this is all I have. Take them boy, and go! Take a horse. God knows there are enough that are now rider-less. Make sure it has a good harness. Ride to the coast.'

'I should stay with you.'

'I am your knight. It is a squire's first duty to obey. Now in the name of God, go! It is my last command.'

Richard leant forward, and kissed Sir Gilbert's sweat-soaked forehead. As he did so the tears started in his eyes, hot and scalding. 'Go on boy,' Sir Gilbert urged gruffly. 'Leave me to God.'

Without a glance back, Richard scrambled out of the ditch. Clutching the saddlebags beneath his cloak the poorest squire in Edward of England's army staggered across the battlefield of Poitiers.

## Medieval Times

Earlier in the day it had been a field of lush green grass. Now it was like hell on earth. A thick mist was rolling across it, as if Nature was trying to hide the horror: decapitated bodies, horses threshing in pain, their iron-shod hooves beating the wounded and the dying, lying as thick as fallen leaves. The cold, misty air was filled with the pain and fear of the wounded.

The sound of fighting had died away. The French were in full retreat, but the English were too exhausted to chase them. Here and there on the battlefield a friar or priest moved among the wounded, offering what comfort they could. Richard stopped one of them and sent him to Sir Gilbert. Plunderers scurried about daggers drawn, finishing off the wounded and stealing from the dead. Richard was stopped several times by English archers, who let him go once they realised he was English. He stopped twice to help the wounded, offering his water bottle to men pleading for a drink. As he did he picked up weapons – a better sword, a dagger – food from a saddlebag and even a cloak, from knights who would no longer need them.

At the edge of the battlefield, Richard found a beautiful black war-horse, shaking its neck and pawing the ground. Now and again it snickered over the corpse lying beside it. Richard pulled the remains of an apple from his purse. The horse took it and allowed Richard to mount. Together they rode off.

The further they travelled from Poitiers, the more the great English victory of Poitiers raised demons of its own. Time and again Richard met up with English free companies – mercenaries who were now roaming the countryside plundering, pillaging and raping. Eventually Richard decided to travel by night and sleep by day, keeping away from the black columns of smoke and the smell of burning. Sometimes monks in a small monastery, or people on isolated farms, sold him food and drink and fodder for the horse. But even if people did not help him, no-one attacked him. Mounted and well armed, he looked too dangerous to challenge.

Adapted from *A Tournament of Murders*, by P. C. Doherty.

# *Dangerous Words*

England's peasants, unhappy at the unfairness of their poor wages and high taxes, were in the mood to revolt. John Ball was one of their leaders who spoke out for change and called on the people to march to London to put their case to the king.

'They say he is a wonderful preacher,' the fat woman in the crowd beside me said.

'Aye,' said the tall man beside her, 'but will we be able to hear him from this far back? He may speak with all the tongues of angels, but it will do us no good if we cannot hear him!'

'Have no fear, my master,' said a small, wrinkled friar with a huge, twisted staff. 'You will hear him well enough. And understand him too, which is more than can be said for what you'd hear in there!' He nodded at the church, where many were at that moment attending Mass.

'Now, the clergyman in there,' the friar continued, 'is talking in Latin, though he might as well be speaking the language of the Man in the Moon for all you'd understand it – and for all that most of them in there would understand it. John Ball speaks of God in plain words, and he speaks good sense for all to hear!'

'Well,' said the fat woman good-humouredly, 'how you do run on! You've heard him speak before then?'

'Many times. What he has to say is important. It is a truth that should be heard over and over.'

'If you would hold your tongue, good friar,' interrupted the tall man, 'we might just find out how important what he has to say is, for here he comes!'

I craned my neck and could just make out a figure climbing the steps of the cross in the middle of the market place. He began to speak. The friar was right, we could hear him clearly, despite the mutterings of the crowd, swelling with those leaving the church after Mass.

'My good friends,' John Ball began, 'hear me! I come to speak to you of matters in England. Things do not go well, and I say they never will go well, until all things are in common, by which I mean until all men are

# Medieval Times

## **Dangerous Words**

equal. There should be no lords or peasants, no, the lords should be no more masters than ourselves.'

There was a gasp from the crowd. The friar was nodding his head, agreeing. But many people in the crowd were looking shocked. What did he mean? How could there be no lords, no peasants? I tried hard to understand the idea. There had always been lords and peasants. How could Richard Fitzhugh, lord of my manor, ever work on the land as I did? He wouldn't have the first idea about how to guide a plough, how to manage the oxen, how to sow the seeds. And what about me? How could I run a manor court, fight for the king in war?

'Daft,' snorted the fat woman. 'Plain daft!'

I agreed with her. This John Ball was just a fool after all, and I had walked almost a whole day to hear him speak. He was still speaking: 'Are we not all descended from the same parents, Adam and Eve?'

That was true, I thought.

'And what reason can they give that they should be more masters than ourselves? They wear velvets, silks and fur. We wear scratchy coarse cloth. They have wines, spices, fine breads while we have only coarse rye bread and water. They have handsome homes, we have poor cottages. We have to labour in the fields, braving the wind and rain, and it is our labour that supports them in luxury.'

That's very true, I thought. I remembered working in the fields in the wind and rain and going home to a cottage with a leaky thatch to a meal of coarse bread and nothing else. He was right. It wasn't fair.

John Ball carried on: 'We are slaves, and are beaten if we do not do as we are told. Let us go to the king and speak with him. He is young, maybe he will see reason! We must go to the king and tell him of our problems! He may not know of them, but when he does he might remedy them.'

So he might. Maybe, I thought, the king had been so sheltered that he had no idea of our problems. Maybe he would put things right, once he was made aware of them. John Ball wasn't daft, after all. He was right. We must go to London and ask the king for help. I am not at all sure that I heard his last words correctly over the cheering crowd: 'And if he will not help us, then must we take matters into our own hands.'

Whatever he said, he is right at bottom, not daft. We must go to London to see the king. To London, to set things right.

# Chain Reaction

At the midsummer fair Sam gave his peforming bear just one more prod to make it dance on its paws. For the bear that was one prod too many. It gave an enormous backward kick, went down on all fours and tried to bite a lump from Sam's arm. The backward kick, however, had brought the bear's strong paws into contact with the shaky wooden

# Chain Reaction

supports of Martha Goodfellow's stocking booth. It collapsed, burying Martha amongst her stockings and socks. John the Potter was knocked unconscious and the people surrounding his table were showered with shards of broken jugs and bowls. The sheep, terrified, rampaged through and around the stalls and booths. Worse was to come …

# *The Woolpack*

It is 1493. Thomas Fetterlock is a respected wool merchant in the town of Burford, in the Cotswolds. But the wool trade is in decline. It is only because of loans from the Lombard bankers that Thomas has been able to keep his business afloat. Thomas' son, Nicholas, discovers something sinister and tries to solve a mystery involving the Lombards.

Simon Leach's barn was certainly in a desolate spot. Nicholas rode his pony Petronel across the line of the hill and approached the barn from above. Simon was a wool-packer who worked for Nicholas' father, who was a wool merchant. Nicholas knew his father did not pay generous wages. So, how could a mere wool-packer own a barn? And what did he keep in it? He noticed a couple of horses tethered to a corner of the building. One of them was Leach's piebald mare. Then out through the barn doors came Leach and another man. Nicholas drew a sharp breath. He would have recognised those high black shoulders anywhere. It was the Lombard bankers' secretary. The man with the face like a toad.

The two men stood outside in the sunlight for a couple of minutes examining a woollen fleece which they held in their hands. Then they went back into the barn.

❊ ❊ ❊

Later, Nicholas told Cecily what he had seen. She nodded thoughtfully. 'Shall I tell you a strange thing that happened? After the man you call Toad-face killed my kitten I had bad dreams every night. My father took me away with him to stay with my grandmother. She lives in the New Forest. One morning I was out with my cousins. Toad-face was riding, just riding through the Forest, at the end of a string of packhorses.'

'I suppose he was going to Southampton,' Nicholas hazarded. 'The Lombard ships lie at Southampton.'

'It was miles from Southampton,' retorted Cecily. 'No one could possibly go to Southampton that way. I told my father about it, but he only said that the comings and goings of the Lombards were a mystery too great for him to solve.' She leaned towards Nicholas and lowered her voice. 'Do you know,' she whispered, 'I hate that horrible man. I believe he is the Devil come to earth. I'd like to throw some holy water at him just to see if it would sizzle.'

## The Woolpack

But Nicholas' mind was busy with more practical matters. 'Are you sure he was alone?' he persisted. 'Messer Antonio was not with him?'

She shook her head. 'There was a man with him but it was not Messer Antonio. It was a strange man. He was riding a piebald horse.'

Nicholas almost shouted at her. 'A piebald horse? A black and white one? Are you certain?'

'Quite certain,' she answered. 'I always wish when I see a piebald horse. We all wished – my cousins, too.' She stopped as she saw Nicholas' face. 'Why, is there anything the matter?'

Nicholas answered slowly and solemnly. 'I rather think there is,' he said.

❋ ❋ ❋

Nicholas and Giles were talking. Giles was one of his father's shepherds and a great friend to Nicholas since they were small children. Giles reported that the shearing was going well. Leach and his team of hired men had sorted the wool as it was cut, and most of it was graded and packed already. Almost all the wool was good enough to go to Calais, and thirty sacks were packed for Southampton, for the Lombards. Giles spat with deliberation as he mentioned them. Then he glanced over his shoulder to make sure they were alone.

'I am not happy about things, Nicholas. Tomorrow I must see your father. Last week I caught one of the packers cutting the feet and legs off a whole sheepskin and folding it in a sack to pass as clipped wool. He was new, one of Leach's men. So I opened another sack and found

## Medieval Times

it had fine wool on the top and was stuffed with rubbish underneath, all sewn up into sacks with the best Arras canvas and thread, and sealed with your father's guild mark.'

'Did you tell Leach about it?' asked Nicholas.

'On my life I did. He sent the man about his business there and then. If I'd had my way he'd have gone before the justices and spent a day in

## *The Woolpack*

the pillory, but Leach said that it wouldn't be good for our name if these things became known. He is the packer. It is his business, so I had no more to say.'

Nicholas was thinking deeply. 'You say that the man had stuffed the sack with a sheepskin? Where did he get the sheepskin? We don't kill sheep when they are clipped.'

Giles chuckled with appreciation. 'You are a bright one, sir. That's the very thing I asked Leach. He said that he had an order for a pack of sheepskins and he had got some out of his barn.'

'Then he has got wool in his barn,' cried Nicholas triumphantly.

'What he has in his barn is known only to the blessed saints', returned the shepherd, 'but I think it's about time that others knew as well. Leach has business with the Lombards; we know that, and I don't trust the man.'

It was on the tip of Nicholas' tongue to mention the meeting between Leach and the Lombards in the New Forest but he controlled the impulse. 'You will tell my father about this?' he urged.

'He will know in the morning,' vowed Giles fervently. 'Tonight he will be tired after his journey, but I'll go and see him by eight in the morning.'

**Adapted from *The Woolpack*, by Cynthia Harnett.**

# *Harry Bailey's Inn*

In the 14th century all sorts of people travelled to Canterbury to visit the Cathedral and pay homage at the shrine of Thomas Becket, the Archbishop of Canterbury murdered by the knights of Henry II. Here the landlord of an inn in London watches the pilgrims prepare for their journey.

All day long the pilgrims have been arriving. Tall ones, short ones, fat ones, thin ones, and the odd smelly one too. I'm sure there are even more here than last year. I always know when that time of year is coming around again – the flowers start showing their faces, the birds wake up in the trees and sing their little hearts out, and folk decide to go on pilgrimages. I'm not sure if it's because they want to make their peace with God and start afresh with the spring, or if it's just because it's finally stopped raining and the weather's right for a ride in the country!

Still, whatever the reason, they always seem to gather here in my inn, The Tabard in Southwark, before heading off for Canterbury together at first light. Funny old lot, they are. I remember last year, the night before they left, a merchant and a reeve got into a brawl about some game of cards. Fists started flying, beer everywhere, the women shrieking for the men to behave, and then next morning, they all set off, pious as you like, as if nothing had happened!

Well whatever, it's good news for me, as they all need supper, ale and a bed for the night before they go – I've got twenty-two booked in already and they're still arriving. I wish I'd asked Edith to work today, I could have one with the help.

'A hogshead of your finest ale please Harry. It's time my son got a taste for it. Might turn him into a real man, rather than a lady's man!'

It was the knight. Of course I knew it was the knight because he was in armour, but I'd have known anyway. He comes here every year, and always with skin as nut-brown as a haymaker's in August. The rest of us were still whiter than white from the cold winter past. But the knight spent his life travelling all over the world, to exotic and dangerous countries far away, to fight for our religion in Crusades. It's said he's been in fifteen battles, and killed many a man. His son has not inherited his father's religious honour. He is a squire, and a real womaniser, but clever enough to hide it behind romance. His blonde curls and fresh face make him look angelic, but I've heard his midnight

## Harry Bailey's Inn

footsteps every year, pitter-patter away from his father's room and into the room of some lady or another. Tut tut!

'Master Bailey – may I just enquire as to when our food will arrive? My hunger makes me weak.'

The prioress's voice startled me and made guilt hammer on my head for thinking such lewd thoughts. She was a proper servant of the Church. Unlike the Friar.

'Food's on it's way Madam Prioress, worry not.'

The whole group was growing hungry by now, and I wished the food would hurry up as they were all starting to get restless. All but one pleasant but serious-looking man, who spent most of his time watching the others, and writing in a small pocket-book. He must have been a learned man. He certainly knew his letters.

'Oi, Master Chaucer.'

The Friar had woken up from his dozing and was bellowing at the quiet man with the pocket book.

'That is your name isn't it?'

The regular members of the group were used to the Friar. Used to the fact that he would regularly be drunk before the sun was high in the sky, and that he may have fallen in some ditch in a drunken stupor before the sun had set. The new members, however, seemed a little shocked to see a man of the cloth behaving in this way. He continued:

'My name is Hubert the Friar, and I'm pleased to meet you. You may not be aware that it is customary for new members of the group to sup ale with the Friar, to better make his acquaintance before we travel to Canterbury.'

The Friar grinned widely at the stranger, revealing a line of yellow and broken teeth. Chaucer nodded politely.

'So I'll have a mug of Harry's finest, thanking you Master Chaucer.'

'Oh, pay him no heed Master Chaucer. He is a perfect rogue with a perfect disguise and no mistake. Come here and sit by me and let me introduce myself.'

Now here was someone I looked forward to seeing, year after year. From underneath an enormous hat and wimple the goodwife's wide body and scarlet-stockinged legs poked out. She lifted her head and

## Medieval Times

smiled the gap-toothed smile that I remembered from years back. Here was someone who could give the Friar a run for his money!

## Harry Bailey's Inn

'Goodwife of Bath, do not distract the man from his lesson with me. Sure, to sit by the Friar all night will stand him in good stead for his pilgrimage, will it not? Put him in mind of things holy?'

The Wife of Bath tipped her head back and roared with laughter. She laughed so hard and so loud that the general murmur of conversation in the room stopped, and all eyes turned to look at where the noise was coming from. Gasping for breath, the Wife slapped her thigh and spoke between guffaws: 'Things holy? Oh Hubert, there are many things that you put me in mind of – but holy things they are certainly not!'

Just then the food arrived, and in his eagerness to eat, the Friar quite forgot to take offence at the Wife's words. I could tell Chaucer was relieved that attention was off him for a while. He had started to look quite uncomfortable with it all.

## Medieval Times

Slurps, squelches and grunts took the place of chatter in the room while the pilgrims ate their vittels. Fine fowl and rabbit, roasted in honey by the cook, and served on trenchers of bread. All ate with great enjoyment, and great noise.

Just then, the Friar let out an enormous belch, which silenced the group instantly. I seized the moment of quiet to talk to them. 'Good pilgrims. I am pleased indeed to see you all returning to my tavern this year, and not to the Bell next door! You all seem in the mood for fun, and so I have an idea to put to you. Many a year have I heard your stories, some true, some not, but all entertaining. Many a year have I considered riding with you to Canterbury, to hear more of your tales. Well, this year I will ride, and I will suggest good sport too.

'Let each pilgrim tell two stories on the way to Canterbury, and two on the way back. Whoever tells the best tale shall have his dinner bought for him by the others when we return. I shall be the judge of the stories, and the judge's word is final. If anyone tries to contest my ruling, they must pay for everything bought by everybody along the way. What think you all of this plan?'

In their mood of drunken happiness, all the pilgrims agreed enthusiastically to the plan, and then, boasting of what their story would be, they one by one took themselves off to bed.

Early next morning, when it was still quite dark, I set about giving the wake-up call to the sleepy pilgrims. We had to start early on our way, but the enthusiasm from the night before was now sorely lacking. Hangovers were making many curse last night's drunkenness. I tried to jolly them along the way. 'Not far now to Saint Thomas' watering place, and there I suggest we stop, drink a little, eat a little, and draw straws for who will tell the first tale.'

Around the next corner the watering place came into sight and I started cutting shoots from the trees so we could draw straws. All stood around while their horses drank, and I held out the straws in my fist. All drew, and the knight held up the shortest straw. A good man to start, he looked pleased, and cleared his throat. While the sunlight started to warm our backs, we ate and drank and listened to the knight's gentle voice.

'Once on a time, as old tales tell to us, there was a duke whose name was Theseus...'

**Adapted from *The Canterbury Tales*, by Geoffrey Chaucer**